Illustrations credits:

Archivio White Star/Marcello Bertinetti:
Cover, back cover, 1, 7, 8-9, 10-11, 12-13, 17, 18, 22, 30-31, 33, 34, 37, 40-41, 42-43, 46-47, 48, 52-53, 54-55, 66, 72-73, 74, 76, 88-89, 90, 94-95.
Archivio White Star/Carlo De Fabianis:
2-3, 6, 14-15, 19, 28-29, 35, 39, 49, 50, 57, 64-65, 70-71, 91, 92-93.
Archivio White Star/Angela White Bertinetti:
4, 6, 20-21, 24-25, 32, 36, 38, 44-45, 51, 56, 58-59, 67, 68-69, 77 top, 77 bottom left, 96.
Antonio Attini:
60, 61, 62-63.
Guido Borsani:
84, 85.
Cesare Gerolimetto:
24, 65, 75, 77 bottom right, 79, 82, 83, 86.
Fulvio Roiter/Overseas:
23, 25, 78, 80-81, 87, 92.

First published in English in 1991 by Tiger Books International PLC, London.

This 1991 edition published by Crescent Books, distributed by Outlet Book Company, Inc.
A Random House Company
225 Park Avenue South
New York
New York 10003

ISBN 0-517-05880-4
87654321

INSIDE VENICE

TEXT
PAOLO FONTANA

DESIGN
PATRIZIA BALOCCO

CRESCENT BOOKS
New York

Why is it that Venice appears different from all other cities in the world? One answer could be that the city is made not only of stone, water and air, but is a combination of all these elements. They interact to form a splendid edifice of light, colour and form which is re-invented daily with changes in perspective, the time of day and the seasons. The marvellous uniqueness of its structure makes Venice the place where everyone would like to live or at least spend a part of their existence. Surrounded by the sea, it appears touchingly fragile: a dream made of marble and of dull, almost threatening, skies; a fascinating marvel, built on millions of wooden poles by an indomitable people who represented the last bulwark against the assault of an uncivilised epoch.

The first town plan of the city was probably traced by the course of the river Brenta which was prevented from flowing into the sea by the opposing thrust of the Adriatic. Originally, the Canal Grande (Grand Canal) was nothing other than the final stretch of the course of the river which snaked its way between islands of mud on its way from the lagoon to the sea. Venice had still to be founded, and all that existed were sparse settlements of fishermen scattered along the coast and in the lagoon area. Around the turn of the 5th century, the new centres of Grado Eraclea, Concordia and Torcello were founded. Waves of refugees abandoned the ancient but insecure cities of Aquileia, Altino and Caorle, which had been devastated by barbarian invaders, and congregated around the shores of the large lagoon, squashed between the mouth of the Brenta and the Malamocco coastline. They immediately felt the need to provide

themselves with a government and first they elected maritime tribunes who were dependent on the Exarch of Ravenna, and then a "Doge" who established himself first at Malamocco, before moving to the safer zone of Rialto.

The 120 small islands became united little by little as long tree trunks were driven into the sediment, providing foundations for wooden houses; 450 large and small bridges were built to connect houses, streets and squares.

The first Doge of the city was elected in 726 and, from then on, Venice really became an island of happiness which looked on as the rest of the peninsula was devastated by the Ostrogoths. It was to flee from an umpteenth invasion, that of Charlemagne's son Pepin in the year 800, that the Venetians founded the fortified heart of Venice. Only 20 years later, this people, who possessed great independence of spirit, were building a basilica to house the sacred mortal remains of Saint Mark, purloined from Alexandria in Egypt and brought to the lagoon after an adventurous voyage. The relic was accompanied by a symbol, a winged lion with a proud and radiant gaze. This wild beast became the symbol of the new power that kings and popes, emperors and caliphs would have to learn to take account of. The splendid liberty of Venice transformed it into a republic of oligarchs and this guaranteed it complete autonomy.

As her trade increased, the power of the city also grew, to the point where Venice controlled the Mediterranean. Venice, the trading power, established bases at all the strategic points along the trade routes, also thanks to her subtle diplomacy. On these shores, Venice was establishing herself as one of the four great

PAX | EVAN
TIBI | GELI
MAR | STA
CE | MEVS

10-11 In the vicinity of Rialto Bridge striped poles rise up from the canal bottom ready to receive the prows of boats wanting to moor here.

12-13 The gondolas rest after a day's work. In the background, from the right, are the Chiesa della Salute, the Punta della Dogana and the Chiesa del Redentore on the island of Giudecca.

Maritime Republics which were to guarantee three centuries of prosperity and peace. Then, conflicts arose, especially with Genoa and with the Turks. Once more Venice came out triumphant and invaded Constantinople in 1204. The great victory over the Byzantines gave the city the celebrated bronze horses of St. Mark's Cathedral and other treasures which, to this day, are housed in the Basilica. The greatness of Venice in this period led to the formation of an enormous coalition against it: a league, created with the intention of humiliating the golden lion. The major powers of the old continent, urged on by Pope Julius II, put a stop to Venetian expansion, while the Turks took their revenge in the city's oriental domains. But the real decadence set in after the discovery of America which became the focal point of European commercial interests. It was the beginning of the slow but glorious decline of an empire which still managed to resist the Moors at Candia and Cyprus, to re-conquer part of Greece, and to defeat the Barbers at Tunis towards the end of the 18th century. Only Napoleon humiliated that which was left of the maritime myth by selling off the Republic to Austria. It was only a momentary lapse: a few years later, that courage which had always animated the lagoon, re-exploded with the short but heroic Republic of Daniele Manin in 1849.

The city had asked to be Italian but, perhaps more than anything else, to be free again. In 1866 with the Third War of Italian Independence, it became part of the Kingdom of Italy without however losing that longing for freedom which has made it famous throughout the world.

14 The statue of St. George rises up to protect the Lagoon.

14-15 In full daylight the Doges' Palace appears in all its majesty, a blend of Byzantine, Gothic and Renaissance styles.

16 St. Mark's Basilica, with its Gothic-style marble groups and Byzantine-style mosaics.

17 The simplicity of St. Mark's Bell Tower rises above the marble arabesques of the Doges' Palace.

17

18-19 The Ca'd'Oro is a typical example of 15th-century Gothic architecture and was designed by the Lombardian architect Matteo Reverti and the Bon brothers. The Palace owes its name to the no longer visible gilding which covered its marble facade.

*B*ecause of its very structure, which cannot be influenced by town-planners, Venice has preserved the appearance it had in the 13th century. Even the names of the streets and the squares are those of bygone times: "calli" are the narrow alleyways running between the houses; "sakizade" were the first paved streets; "fondamenta", a street bordering a canal; "rii", the smaller canals; "rii terra", canals which have been covered over, while "campi " and "campielli" are the larger and smaller squares which suddenly open up before the visitor, especially in the middle of the major islands. The only "Piazza" is St. Mark's Square, the heart of the city which pulsates around the stupendous Basilica. This complex of buildings seems to be a figment of the imagination of a bizarre and confused, but genial, architect. Seen from all sides, this splendid assortment of forms provides incredible perspectives with its multi-coloured facades and its contrasting golds.
Its actual appearance is the result of a series of re-workings and the superimposition of styles, dating from the original construction which Pietro Orseolo wanted to house the relic of the Evangelist, up to the ultimate consecration of 1703. Exarchial architectural forms, merged with parts of Byzantine inspiration, are grafted on to material from a much earlier date. There are columns, and groups of statues which originated in the ancient or Imperial Roman period. Brilliant Moorish inlays, as well as Gothic, Oriental and Renaissance mosaics and decorative elements, are also present. It is to this casual, yet harmonious, fusion of styles that St. Mark's Basilica owes its fantastic appearance; it is a work of art which has no equal in

20-21 A group of statues situated at the edge of the Doges' Palace. On the left is the bridge of Sighs which was built in 1589 by Antonio da Ponte, the same architect who built the Rialto Bridge. Condemned prisoners passed directly from the court to the prisons across this bridge.

the European artistic heritage.

Externally, the facade offers an unforgettable spectacle with its naive and fascinating medieval encyclopedia representing the months, and the virtues and crafts of man. The interior is a treasure-house: magnificent mosaics, icons and frescoes take the visitor on a voyage to the Paleo-Christian Orient. A mystic atmosphere enfolds the beholder, who is faced with a succession of motifs that recall the simplicity of Romanesque or the sumptuousness of Gothic style.

Naturally, Venice is not just St. Mark's. Every Venetian can tell you that the most authentic and meaningful way to get to know the city is to follow itineraries far from the beaten tourist track. To find one's way among the many "calli" and "campielli" is rather difficult, yet, it is here that one can experience the charm of the city. In Venice one often finds oneself wandering about with no particular destination, almost as if instinctive powers had been reawakened. The imagination guides the sensitivity of the wayfarer who humbly approaches these stones steeped in glory and melancholy beauty, and makes him aware of the particular atmosphere which hangs in the air, a singular mixture of eternal changelessness and insidious precariousness. Thus we can discover the most hidden corners and satisfy a curiosity stimulated by the austere facades of the palaces.

This hidden Venice can also expose the visitor to the acrid smell of the canals and the water which laps the edges of the houses that are green with algae. Turning again towards the centre of the city, we file past the Gothic fascination of Ca'd'Oro, the Byzantine motifs of Cà Farsetti and the simple Renaissance

harmony of the Scala a Bovolo (the spiral staircase).
Starting out from Santa Lucia, on one of the many boats which take one to the middle of the city, one comes into contact with the overwhelming beauty of this open-air museum, and little by little, one begins to recognise those special emotions that will always be associated with memories of Venice. Thus, for anyone who visits it, this city becomes an endless source of unique sensations. Venturing among the thousand canals teaches us that true beauty, incorporated in these sculpted stones, is ageless. The threatening lagoon which surrounds Venice insinuates itself into the cracks in the ancient marble but it cannot destroy the allure of the city's contrasts, softened by the slow rhythm beaten out by the clocks of the bell-towers, each one different from the next, and all pointing heaven-wards, invoking eternity.

22 The austere statues of St. Mark's Basilica stand out clearly against the light blue sky.

23 An aerial view of the city. The white lines which once marked out the spaces set aside for the stalls of the various vendors can still be seen in Piazza San Marco.

24 *A panoramic view of St Mark's Basin: at the bottom, the Canale della Giudecca is visible, while at the top, the cemetery and the island of Murano can be seen.*

25 *A charming picture of St. Mark's Basin and the Island of San Giorgio.*

25

26 Stunning decorative details embellish the entrance and the facade of the Doges' Palace.

27 Across the square from St. Mark's Bell Tower, the Clock Tower stands out. It is surmounted by two "Moors" who have been striking the hours for five centuries.

28 An unusual glimpse of café tables in St. Mark's Square.

29 The appeal of the pigeons in St. Mark's Square is irresistible, especially for children.

30-31 Caffè Chioggia, in the Piazzetta San Marco, is one of the busiest meeting places in the city.

32 The statue of the saint and the mosaics on the
facade of St. Mark's Basilica are lit by the rays of
the setting sun.

33 The aggressive winged lion has always been the symbol of the power and charm of Venice.

33 The aggressive winged lion has always been the symbol of the power and charm of Venice.

34 A new perspective on St. Mark's Basilica lightly covered with snow.

34-35 The interior of St. Mark's Basilica with its mixture of Byzantine motifs and late Gothic lines.

36

36 This beautiful spiral staircase was built by Giovanni Candi in 1499 in the Lombardian style.

37 The bronze horses of San Marco were brought to Venice from Constantinople by the Doge Enrico Dandolo in 1204.

*I*f anyone were to wonder why Venice is the city of lovers, the answer would doubtless be found in the bewitching light of the buildings and sunsets, and in the festivals. The lights which envelop the city are extremely varied: there is the natural light which comes to life and fades over the lagoon and the multi-coloured roofs of the city; there is the light of the painters who have frescoed the religious buildings, and the light entering through mullioned and Gothic windows which changes with the seasons. There is also the faint light of alleyways and houses which seem to disdain electric light or, at least, to tone it down a little. The gloomy, harsh colour of the sea is immortalized in the works of Tintoretto and Titian. The mildness of bygone centuries is reflected in the salons, enlivened by candlelight during the many parties which have been given since time immemorial. Those who visit this city are particularly fond of the restful atmosphere of Venetian light, the absence of tension, the streaks of grey and the time-worn white of the marble which merges with the pavements.

This is the other secret of Venice. The large amount of greyness which we encounter in our everyday lives is different here: it is more alive and more natural; a choice, not an imposition. It is the grey of glass rather than that of asphalt walls. Then there is the gold of the sunset and the cupolas; a sky which, in its myriad hues, renders the facades of the city even more beautiful. In Venice, both in St. Mark's Square and in the small squares, one has the impression of being in a house which contains many unknown, yet familiar, rooms. All of a sudden, in a sharp contrast to the soft colours, we come across the

shining light of mosaics, windows and the street-lamps which radiate a muted yellow light; and we have the impression of a reflected energy and brilliance that releases colour and flashes of light.

When illuminated, Venice is the artist's ideal: you never see blinding flashes of light or distressing patches of darkness. This is the home of harmony and of architectural and artistic taste. The lights most charged with colour are turned on for the grand Venetian festivals: in February there is Carnival, which, with its rich masques, brings to life the splendours of the 17th century; there is the beautiful Regatta Storica at the end of the summer when the humid heat has given way to an indefinable coolness which is a prelude to the icy winter winds. Great shows of colour also appear for the "Marriage with the Sea", a ceremony in which a man dressed as a Doge leads a water-borne procession. The soft tones of Venice are on show again for the Festa del Redentore on the third Sunday of July and in the mythical and sarcastic Harlequin, an almost diabolical figure who runs away along the "calli" followed by the notes of an air by Vivaldi. Without doubt it is Vivaldi who writes the score for musical walks in Venice, where the magic tones of romantic emotion and strong passion pursue each other.

38 One of the glorious interiors of the Doges' Palace.

39 The golden staircase of the Doges' Palace was designed by Sansovino and decorated by Alessandro Vittoria.

40 *The Clock Tower shines in the nocturnal light. It was designed at the end of the 15th century and the building was completed in 1755. The zodiac clockface indicates the course of the stars and planets as well as the time.*

41 *The soft and still uncertain light of dawn adds a subtle charm to the Doges' Palace and the cupolas of St. Mark's.*

42-43 Warm and romantic lighting highlights the beauty of Palazzo Dario.

44-45 The "Teatro della Fenice" was built between 1790 and 1792 by Antonio Da Selva. It was seriously damaged by fire in 1836 and restored by the Meduna brothers.

*I*n Venice everything expresses the city's individuality, and one ought not to be surprised that the city has "invented" a very special means of transport for the movement and transport of people and goods. The result of a practised and ancient art, the gondola is still the true and perhaps slightly abused symbol of this maritime city. Its elongated form strikes the eye as does its silent progress along the majestic Grand Canal or the smallest half-hidden "rio". It also has a unique historical origin. The gondola was the Venetians' first means of transport: the most modest type served for the transport of the poorer families, while the rich and the nobility competed with each other to show off the most splendid, colourful ones, embellished with family coats-of-arms, covered with sumptuous canopies and with damask-lined cabins. Only in 1562 did an ordinance of the Doge impose black for everyone, penalizing the desire for sumptuousness which was not in line with the new 17th-century climate of moderation.

So the gondola became dark and, since then, it has conserved all its traditional features: the length, which must be exactly 11 metres (36 feet), and above all the famous and characteristic "pettine", the iron decoration on the bows which ennobles the appearance as well as giving more stability to the vessel. The iron "pettine" has six "teeth" representing the six "sestieri" which make up the entire city: San Marco, Castello, Dorsoduro, San Paolo, Santa Croce and finally Cannaregio. The sides of the hull are asymmetric: in fact, the right side is narrower than the left and the characteristic inclination of the gondola is due precisely to this difference in proportion.

52 Fish market in Rialto.

52-53 The market in Via Garibaldi is one of the most picturesque in the city.

54-55 In Venice, even the markets live on the water. The photograph shows a large transport boat loaded with fruit and vegetables along Rio di San Barnaba.

The gondola is unique and so is the gondolier, who with a single flat, long oar effortlessly guides the craft through the narrowest canals with relaxed movements and an extraordinary familiarity gained through years of patient learning.

The charm of the gondola begins with its elaborate construction; every piece is different from the next and they are made using eight different types of wood. Their design is based on precise calculations which have remained unchanged throughout the centuries and guarded by the few craftsmen who assemble the woods in San Trovaso in the district of Dorsoduro and pass on their craft from one generation to the next.

Snaking its way along the narrowest and quietest "rii", one soon realizes that the gondola takes one back to bygone times when motors had not broken the spell of nature's silence.

50 In the foreground is a bridge over Rio di Palazzo while the Bridge of Sighs can be seen in the background.

51 Even the complicated operations involved in moving house must take place on water, via the canals.

56 One of the typical narrow "calli" (alleyways).

57 The light of the setting sun illuminates St. Mark's Square.

58 Typical houses along "fondamenta" (a street bordering a canal) delle Zattere, a district in Venice.

59 The warm tones of sunset highlight the architectural beauty of the Church of San Giorgio.

*T*radition and history are the main characteristics of Venice, and of its people. Today there are very few real Venetians because they have been chased away from the centre by speculation and tourism. Those who remain have barricaded themselves in their houses. These are people who have never lost the spirit of the ancient merchants nor their particular way of considering themselves special, absolute masters of the most unusual city in the world. Everything in the lives of these people expresses their autonomy and independence: their culture and their cuisine; their manner of living and of spending their free time.

Venice and her inhabitants represent the meeting of different, even distant cultures merged together in a vital and fascinating symbiosis. Oriental remnants and Central European customs find their meeting place here.

Every day, the great history of the "Serenissima" (the Italians' affectionate nickname for Venice) mingles with the commonplace, which in its turn, is ennobled. The sumptuous Carnival and the Vogalonga also form part of everyday life: the myth comes down to earth and mingles with the simple joie de vivre of the local inhabitants, and it is this which attracts crowds who are not always conscious of walking on history or of its fragile nature.

In this city-monument, which lives on its past, folklore and customs are a part of everyday life, the festivals are really lived and have no need to be re-invented to satisfy the demands of today. Carnival and the Regatta in costume are joyful outbursts of colour. In such moments as these, the true Venetian comes to the surface and for a short time forgets his normally introverted, seafaring character.

The true Venetians who once wrested land from the lagoon are now involved in everyday tasks: in shabby gondolas which transport them from one canal to the next and, in moments of tranquillity sitting over a glass of wine and a pack of cards in bars in some anonymous part of the city, always ready to make a cutting remark.

Even the most casual observer will notice the unique rhythms of Venice. Stress and speed are not of these parts: here time passes without hurry in the street, and can be appreciated in the conscientious and precise work of the craftsmen, who labour in the cafés and the kitchens.

On the subject of Venetian cuisine, the gastronomy of the lagoon is not so much based on elaborate dishes as on the passion of those who cook them and that is why there is no fast food. Once again the explanation can be found in history. The women who waited for the men, sons and husbands who had gone to sea, were forced to pass the time working at pillow-lace or producing a cuisine based on interminable cooking times. The "brodetto di pesce" (fish soup) and "sarde in saor" (a sardine dish) are the clearest examples of food inspired by the sea: things which are apparently simple yet refined and tasty. This city, so marvellously isolated from the furious and excessive rhythms of modern life, imposes its own time-scale on those who visit it.

Speed is the demon which could destroy Venice and with it the desire to transform it into a city cum shop-window, constantly

providing it with more services and technology. Progress is rearing its head in the most beautiful city in the world. Noise, overcrowding and indifference could bring to an end the gentle rhythms we have described. The splendid, melancholy spirit of the city is today turning into sadness, into a regal and orderly abandonment. Will Venice survive?

Yet, there is the hope of a new birth. Venice is asking for help from those who really appreciate it. It is asking us to respect the equilibrium which has made it great over the course of the centuries. Venice has always been a perfect illusion come to life, and it is thus that we should like to leave it for those who will come after us: a shining and very human heritage.

60-61 The Venetian Carnival has remote origins. From the beginning of the 15th century, the young nobles formed groups called "Compagnie de Calza" which had the task of organizing the carnival celebrations. Even today the tradition of wearing masks continues, with spectacular displays by people in costume. For several days the face of the city changes completely, taking it back to the splendours of the earlier times.

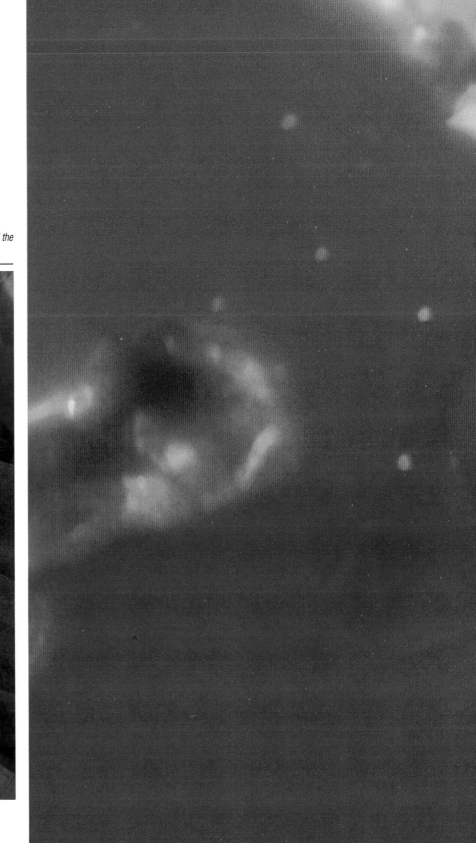

64-65 In the old craft workshops, the masks are still made by hand in the traditional manner from leather, papier mâché, beeswax and water-colours.

66 Rialto Bridge, situated in the middle of the ancient banking and trading quarter, acts as the backdrop to a slow-moving gondola.

67 The profession of gondolier has been handed down through the centuries.

70 There is no doubt that the gondola is the most suitable vessel in which to discover the hidden corners of the city.

71 With extraordinary ability, the gondoliers manoeuvre and row their boats using only one oar.

72-73 In Rio San Trovaso one can still visit a typical "squero", an ancient boat-yard in which gondolas are built and repaired.

76 The piece of iron on the prow of the gondola does not have a merely decorative function but also plays a role in the equilibrium of the gondola by counterbalancing the weight of the gondolier. The six "teeth" of this "pettine" (comb) represent the six "sestrieri", or areas into which the city is divided.

77 Decorative elements embellish the more beautiful gondolas.

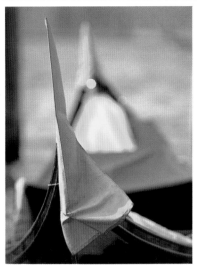

*T*he sight of Venice under a blanket of snow is becoming increasingly rare, almost a privilege of bygone winters. The city, already fabulously unreal, becomes even more fascinating when it is covered in snow. Under a scattering of white flakes, the city appears more restful, the activity along the canals slows down and the gondolas sway gently at their moorings. People and things finally enjoy the tranquillity which is normally upset by mass tourism, which is concentrated mainly in the warmer seasons. In the inns and in their homes, the last remaining Venetians re-discover the old-world atmosphere, and gaze at empty calli and campielli in which the diffused light of the street-lamps is toned down by the whiteness of the snow.
The snow adds a nip to the air, makes the colours brighter, deepens the contrasts of light and dark in the porticoes and the sombre loggias. The rare visitors know that this is the most pleasurable season to visit Venice because one can avoid being harassed. One can combat the biting chill with one of the many hot drinks served in the welcoming Venetian cafés: exquisite interludes around a table, while outside, an almost spiritual silence makes time seem to go more slowly and the sound of footsteps is deadened by the snow. To experience Venice in the snow takes one beyond the idea of winter as a renunciation: instead it can be invigorating and relaxing, even a celebration. Venice in winter gives one a chance to admire the city at leisure; moreover, the snow not only covers up but also uncovers, in terms of revealing the true essence of the place.
Leaving the city, one hopes it might always remain like this: protected and immobile in the cold and in time.

80-81 Snow highlights the beauty of the architectural lines of the Doges' Palace.

82 *Gondolas resting in the snow.*

83 *Orselo Basin, the closest landing stage to St. Mark's Square, after a snowfall.*

84-85 *"Acqua alta" (high water) in Piazzetta and Piazza San Marco. This phenomenon is caused by exceptionally high tides which, in certain meteorological conditions, rise so much that they flood streets and squares.*

86-87 The historical Regatta is held along the Grand Canal in the first week of September every year and it is an event which the entire population looks forward to.

88-89 The boats in St. Mark's Basin are waiting for the starter's gun to begin the Vogalonga. This competition, in which thousands of Venetians row round the city perimeter, was begun in 1975.

90-91 Although it is not linked to an ancient tradition, the Vogalonga provokes great popular enthusiasm and a keen spirit of competition.

92-93 A fantastic fireworks display concludes the celebrations for the "Festa del Redentore" on the night before the third Sunday in July.

94-95 A magic light illuminates the church of Santa Maria della Salute and the Punta della Dogana.